# YOUR KNOWLEDGE HAS VALUE

- We will publish your bachelor's and master's thesis, essays and papers

- Your own eBook and book - sold worldwide in all relevant shops

- Earn money with each sale

Upload your text at www.GRIN.com
and publish for free

Priyank Shah

# Moving Object Detection Using Background Subtraction Algorithms

GRIN Verlag

**Bibliografische Information der Deutschen Nationalbibliothek:**

Die Deutsche Bibliothek verzeichnet diese Publikation in der Deutschen National-
bibliografie; detaillierte bibliografische Daten sind im Internet über http://dnb.d-
nb.de/ abrufbar.

Dieses Werk sowie alle darin enthaltenen einzelnen Beiträge und Abbildungen
sind urheberrechtlich geschützt. Jede Verwertung, die nicht ausdrücklich vom
Urheberrechtsschutz zugelassen ist, bedarf der vorherigen Zustimmung des Verla-
ges. Das gilt insbesondere für Vervielfältigungen, Bearbeitungen, Übersetzungen,
Mikroverfilmungen, Auswertungen durch Datenbanken und für die Einspeicherung
und Verarbeitung in elektronische Systeme. Alle Rechte, auch die des auszugsweisen
Nachdrucks, der fotomechanischen Wiedergabe (einschließlich Mikrokopie) sowie
der Auswertung durch Datenbanken oder ähnliche Einrichtungen, vorbehalten.

**Imprint:**

Copyright © 2014 GRIN Verlag GmbH
Druck und Bindung: Books on Demand GmbH, Norderstedt Germany
ISBN: 978-3-656-67267-8

**This book at GRIN:**

http://www.grin.com/en/e-book/275108/moving-object-detection-using-background-
subtraction-algorithms

**GRIN - Your knowledge has value**

Der GRIN Verlag publiziert seit 1998 wissenschaftliche Arbeiten von Studenten, Hochschullehrern und anderen Akademikern als eBook und gedrucktes Buch. Die Verlagswebsite www.grin.com ist die ideale Plattform zur Veröffentlichung von Hausarbeiten, Abschlussarbeiten, wissenschaftlichen Aufsätzen, Dissertationen und Fachbüchern.

**Visit us on the internet:**

http://www.grin.com/

http://www.facebook.com/grincom

http://www.twitter.com/grin_com

A Dissertation Report on

# "MOVING OBJECT DETECTION USING BACKGROUND SUBTRACTION ALGORITHMS"

# ABSTRACT

In this thesis we present an operational computer video system for moving object detection and tracking . The system captures monocular frames of background as well as moving object and  to detect tracking and identifies those moving objects. An approach to statistically modeling of moving object developed using Background Subtraction Algorithms. There are many methods proposed for Background Subtraction algorithm in past years. Background subtraction algorithm is widely used for real time moving object detection in video surveillance system. In this paper we have studied and implemented different types of methods used for segmentation in Background subtraction algorithm with static camera. This paper gives good understanding about procedure to obtain foreground using existing common methods of Background Subtraction, their complexity, utility and also provide basics which will useful to improve performance in the future . First, we have explained the basic steps and procedure used in vision based moving object detection. Then, we have debriefed the common methods of background subtraction like Simple method, statistical methods like Mean and Median filter, Frame Differencing and W4 System method , Running Gaussian Average and Gaussian Mixture Model and last is Eigenbackground Model. After that we have implemented all the above techniques on MATLAB software and show some experimental results for the same and compare them in terms of speed and complexity criteria. Also we have improved one of the GMM algorithm by combining it with optical flow method, which is also good method to detect moving elements.

# LIST OF FIGURES

# LIST OF TABLES

# INDEX

# CHAPTER 1

## INTRODUCTION

## 1.1 Objective

Detection of motion is very essential and common step in many surveillance system applications. In these applications, the goal is to obtain very high sensitivity in detection of moving objects with less possible false alarm rates. Background segmentation is one of the famous technique that is commonly used. It works on the intensity difference of the current frame with the background frame. Moving object detection and tracking (D&T) are important steps in object recognition, context analysis and indexing processes for visual surveillance systems etc.. It is a big challenge for researchers to prepare algorithms on which detection and tracking is more suitable for background situation, environment conditions and to determine how accurately object D&T (real-time or non-real-time) is made. There are variety of object D&T algorithms and publications available. On that basis we can compare their performance and evaluate via performance metrics. This report provides a systematic review of these algorithms, their brief description and performance analysis and effectiveness in terms of execution time and memory requirements. When the camera is fixed and the number of targets is small, objects can easily be tracked using simple methods. Computer vision-based methods often provides non-invasive solution. Their applications can be divided into three different groups: Surveillance, control and analysis. The object detection and tracking (D&T) process is a necessary requirement for surveillance applications. The control applications, which uses some parameters to control motion calculations and estimation. These parameters are used to control the relevant vision system. The analysis applications are generally automatic, and used to optimize and diagnose system's performance. For well predefined (namely, annotated) datasets, the object recognition algorithms give good accuracy.

The aim of motion tracking is to detect and track moving objects using a sequence of images. Motion tracking is not only useful for monitoring activity in public places, but it is becoming a key procedure for further analysis of video imagery. For example, information about the location and identity of objects at different points in time is the basis of detecting unusual object movements or coordinated activities e.g. strategic plays in a football game. Object detection in videos involves verifying the presence of an object in image sequences and possibly locating it precisely for recognition. Object tracking is to monitor an object spatial and temporal changes during a video sequence, including its presence, position, size, shape, etc.

In recent years, with the latest technological advancements, off-the-shelf cameras became vastly available, producing a huge amount of content that can be used in various application areas. Among them, visual surveillance receives a great deal of interest nowadays. Until recently, video surveillance was mainly a concern only for military or large-scale companies. However, increasing crime rate, especially in metropolitan cities, necessitates taking better precautions in security-sensitive areas, like country borders, airports or government offices. Even individuals are seeking for personalized security systems to monitor their houses or other valuable assets. So, our objective is to develop some sort of algorithm that will satisfy human requirements in future.

## 1.2 Applications

- Traffic monitoring like counting vehicles, detecting and tracking vehicles.
- Human action recognition like run, walk, jump etc.
- Human-computer interaction
- Object tracking
- Many other computer vision application like digital forensics.
- Optical motion capture
- Content based video coding

## 1.3 Literature Survey

This survey paper reviews briefly research works on object detection and tracking in videos. The definition and tasks of object detection and tracking are first described, and the potential applications are mentioned. Followed is the summation of major research highlights and widely used approaches. In this literature we study about various techniques of moving object detection and tracking Reference is included at the end of the report.

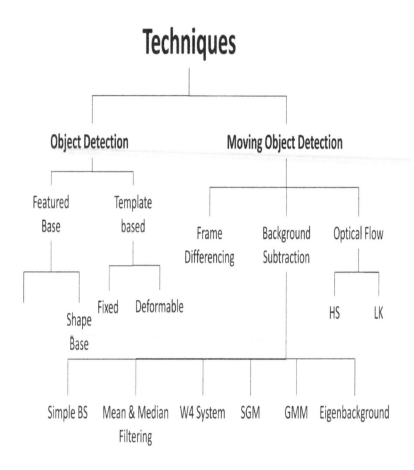

**Fig.1-1 Various Techniques For Object D&T**

Here in this thesis, we are concentrating on moving object detection techniques using background subtraction algorithms [1-5] like Simple Background Subtraction, Mean and Median Filtering. W4 System, Single Gaussian Model, Gaussian Mixture Model and Eigenbackground, their performance and comparison analysis. We have also studied optical flow technique like Horn-Schuck & Lucas-Kanade methods and then by combining it with background subtraction algorithm we can improve our performance specially against false detection due to illumination changes.

## 1-4 Organization of the Report

This report consists of eight chapters in total. The framework for the report is described as follows:

Chapter 1 provides a brief introduction about the basic vision based video surveillance system and the need for an implementation of this report.

Chapter 2 explains the basic concept and principles of the Background Subtraction Algorithm and how the basic operation done to find moving object. It also list some challenges.

Chapter 3 discusses the widely used Background Subtraction Algorithms and it's description, implementation and output analysis .

Chapter 4 gives comparative analysis of methods describe briefly in chapter 3 based on their speed, memory requirement and performance.

Chapter 5 explains the basics of optical flow theory with brief of standard HS algorithm, its procedure to obtain optical flow and its output.

Chapter 6 presents the implementation of combine approach of GMM and Optical Flow and its result comparison with standard GMM output.

Chapter 7 presents the basic HSV threshold approach for shadow detection.

Chapter 8 Finally, I give the reader an overall summary on the collected results and future work.

# CHAPTER 2

## BLOCK DIAGRAM AND CHALLANGES

This chapter contains the basic flow, which is require for the implementation of object detection and tracking. Though these steps can be implemented using many techniques. Also, this chapter explains what are the most common challenges and problems, which must be taken care for good and acceptable results.

### 2.1 General Steps For Object Detection

To perform high level tasks like Video Surveillance, traffic monitoring and Automated event detection, it is necessary to model the background. The performance of these systems is depended on the accuracy and speed of object detection algorithm.

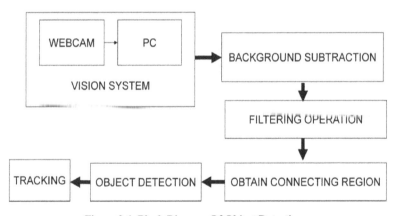

**Figure 2-1 Block Diagram Of Object Detection**

The basic block diagram of object detection procedure is explain in the figure 2-1. The real time image is captured through camera and then using background subtraction algorithm by having a reference background, we can achieve noisy foreground. This noise can be reduce by applying filtering operation, generally Morphological Operation is carried out in this phase. After obtain connecting region, we can able to find foreground mask and ultimately by applying this mask we can detect and track our object. For real time processing Background subtraction algorithm is well suited.

## 2.2 Challenges

There are many challenges to deal with when we have to implement Background Subtraction Algorithm as listed below.

- Illumination changes like clouds moving in the sky
- Motion changes like swaying of trees
- Secondary illumination effects like static shadows
- Moving Shadows and camouflage.

# CHAPTER 3

## STUDY OF DIFFERENT BACKGROUND SUBTRACTION ALGORITHMS

In this chapter we have discussed many commonly used Background Subtraction methods which are highly used for segmentation of given image in order to find foreground mask.

### 3.1 Simple Background Subtraction Method

In basic method for Background subtraction, the static background image without object is taken first as a reference image. After that the current image of the video is subtracted pixel by pixel from the background image and resultant image is converted into binary image using threshold value. This binary image is worked as a foreground mask. For conversion in binary image threshold is required. From [1] we can write

$$|I^t(x,y) - B(x,y)| > T \qquad (1)$$

Where, $I^t(x,y)$ is pixel intensity of frame at time t, B(x,y) is mean intensity on background pixel and T is threshold. When difference reaches beyond threshold the pixel categorize as a foreground pixel.

So the effectiveness of the object detection is depends on the threshold value. Although this method is very fast, it is very sensitive to illumination changes and noise.

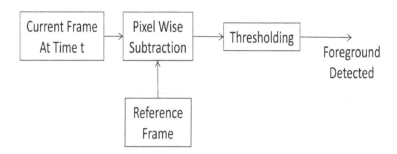

**Figure 3- 1 Block Diagram Of Simple Background Subtraction Method**

Figure 1- 2 Original Video Sequence

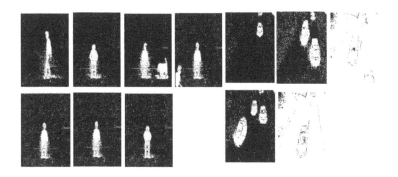

Figure 3- 3 Simple Background Subtraction with Threshold 10

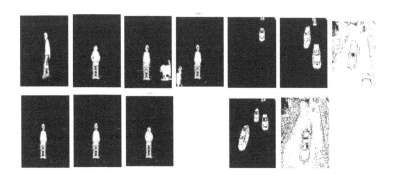

Figure 3- 4 Simple Background Subtraction with Threshold 20

For result analysis we have taken two video sequences [6] from which some of the frames are shown in Figure 3-2. After taking consideration of reference frame we are subtracting each frame from reference frame. Then, we can use threshold T as per equation (1) to obtain binary image as shown in figure 3- 3 for Threshold value 10 and in figure 3-4 for threshold value 20. We can also apply dilution and erosion operation to improve our foreground mask. From comparing results from two threshold we can say that the output mask is very much sensitive to threshold value. Though, this algorithm is fast but also very much sensitive to noise and lightning changes.

## 3.2 Mean Filtering Method

The next method is mean filtering. Figure 3-5 gives as the basic functionality of Mean Filtering. In this method the reference frame is calculated using the mean of the last n frames as per equation 2 given below.

$$B(x, y, t) = \frac{1}{n} \sum_{1}^{n-1} I(x, y, t - i) \qquad (2)$$

where, B(x,y,t) is reference background calculated at time t and I(x,y) is the pixels intensity. So, the foreground can be found using equation 3, where T is a threshold.

$$| I(x,y,t) - B(x,y,t) | > T \qquad (3)$$

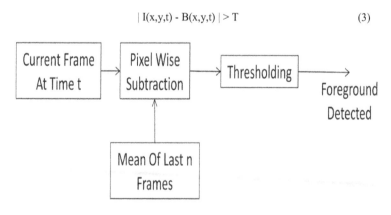

**Figure 3- 5 Block Diagram Of Mean Filtering Algorithm**

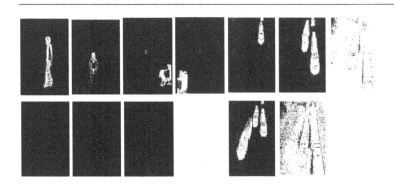

**Figure 3- 2 Mean Filtering With Mean Of 5 Frames**

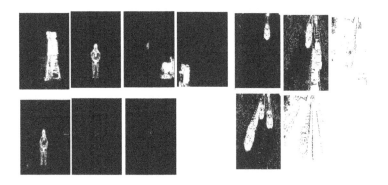

**Figure 3-3 Mean Filtering With Mean Of 15 Frames**

As shown in figure 3-6 & 3-7, we have calculated mean image from last 5 & 15 frames and in order to obtain mask we have subtracted mean image from ith image. we have consider T = 8 for both case. It is easy to implement and adaptive for background calculation. But accuracy is depends on object speed, also memory requirement is very high and have global threshold i.e. same threshold for every pixel. Also from results we can comment that if training signal is too long than memory requirement is very high and if to short than updating rate gets very high. So, slow moving object is not detected property.

## 3.3 Median Filtering Method

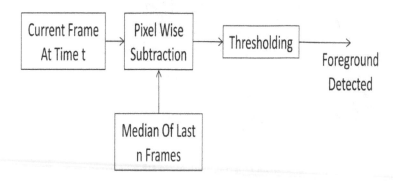

**Figure 3- 8 Block Diagram Of Median Filtering Algorithm**

The another method is median filter. Figure 3-8 gives as the basic functionality of Medeiann Filtering, in which background model B(x,y,t) is given by equation 4.

$$B(x, y, t) = median\ of\ n\ frames\{\ I(x, y, t - i)\} \qquad (4)$$

The advantages of the these two above methods are they are fast, easy to implement and adaptive background calculation. The disadvantages are accuracy is depends on object speed, also memory requirement is very high and global threshold i.e. same threshold for every pixel.

As shown in figure 3-9 & 3-10, we have calculated median image form last 5 & 15

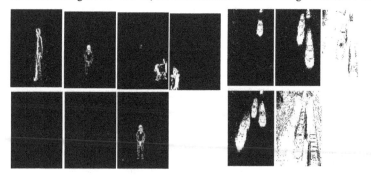

**Figure 3-9 Median Filtering With Mean Of 5 Frames**

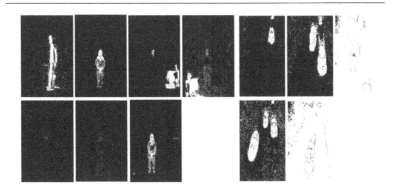

**Figure 3-10 Median Filtering with Mean Of 15 Frames**

frames with T= 8 and in order to obtain mask we have subtracted mean image from ith image. It is easy to implement and adaptive for background calculation. But accuracy is depends on object speed, also memory requirement is very high and have global threshold i.e. same threshold for every pixel. Also from results we can comment that if training signal is too long than memory requirement is very high and if to short than updating rate gets very high. So, slow moving object is not detected property.

## 3.4 W4 System Method

The next method is based on method used in W4 system. As mentioned in [1-2] and [7], we can say, during training sequence maximum intensity, minimum intensity and maximum intensity difference (Dmax) in successive frame of the pixel is calculated and then foreground pixel is calculated based on following equation. Also the basic operation is mentioned in figure 3-11.

$$I^t(x,y) > Imax(x,y) \quad Or$$

$$I^t(x,y) < Imin(x,y) \quad Or \tag{5}$$

$$|I^t(x,y) - I^{t-1}(x,y)| > Dmax(x,y)$$

The disadvantage of this method is it can only be applicable for gray images only and it is not an adaptive method.

The results are shown in figure 3-12. we have taken first 10 frames as training frames

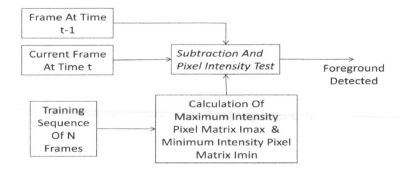

**Figure 3- 11 Block Diagram Of W4 System**

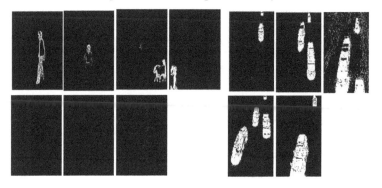

**Figure 3-12 Output Of W4 System**

and using them we have calculated images which contain maximum intensity of every pixel and minimum intensity of every pixel using training frames. After that using this information and intensity variations in to successive frames, we can find mask for moving objects using equation (5) . As output depends on neighboring frames in this technique, output is not so much sensitive to lighting changes and for the same reason the slow moving object is not detected accurately. In this experiment we used T = 10 as threshold.

## 3.5 Frame Differencing Method

The another method is based on frame differing also known as Temporal Differencing. As explain in [3-5], the basic operational block is shown in figure 3-13. In this method moving object is found by taking difference between two or

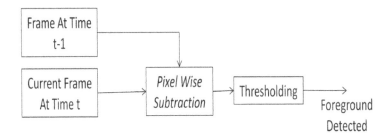

**Figure 3- 13 Block Diagram Of Frame Differencing**

more consecutive frames using following equation.

$$|I_n(x,y) - I_{n-1}(x,y)| > T \qquad (6)$$

The disadvantage is that if the object moves very slowly it might not detect. So, it is only works when object satisfy certain speed criterion. Also, accuracy is very sensitive with the selection of threshold value. This method is based on non-adapting background subtraction. As from figure 3-13 we can say that output depends on

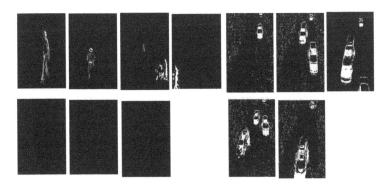

**Figure 3-14  Output Of Frame Differencing**

neighboring frames in this technique, output is not so much sensitive to lighting changes and for the same reason the slow moving object is not detected accurately. In this experiment we used T = 10 as threshold.

## 3.6 Running Gaussian Average Model

The next approach is probabilistic known as Running Gaussian average. We can summaries form[2] and [8] that this approach is generally used with (R, G, B) and (Y, U, V) color spaces. In this model for each pixel location a Gaussian probability density function (pdf) of last n pixel is calculated and then it is compared with current frame. For this mean or average and standard deviation are calculated for each pixel. At time t the running average is given by

$$\mu_t = (1 - \alpha)\mu_{i-1} + \alpha I_t \qquad (7)$$

Where, $I_t$ is current value of pixel, $\mu_t$ is last average and $\alpha$ is the empirical weight, which is useful to give higher weight for current frames and lesser for old frames. Thus, we can update the reference background if changes are not so fast. After computing last average we can distinguish pixels whether it is foreground pixel or background pixel using $\mu_t$ and $\sigma_t$ parameters.

$$|I_t - \mu_t| > k\sigma_t \qquad (8)$$

Where, $\sigma_t$ is a standard deviation at time t. The pixel classified as foreground if it satisfy above equation otherwise it is classify as background. So, from equation(9) , average can be computed without storing to much memory so the it will increases the speed of operation is well.

As by using running average formula it will also consider the foreground region for calculation of average. To eliminate this other formula is suggested.

$$\mu_t = M\mu_{i-1} + (1 - M)((1 - \alpha)\mu_{i-1} + \alpha I_t) \qquad (9)$$

Where M is 1 when it is foreground pixel and 0 for background pixel. This is also known as selective background update method.

## 3.7 Gaussian Mixture Model

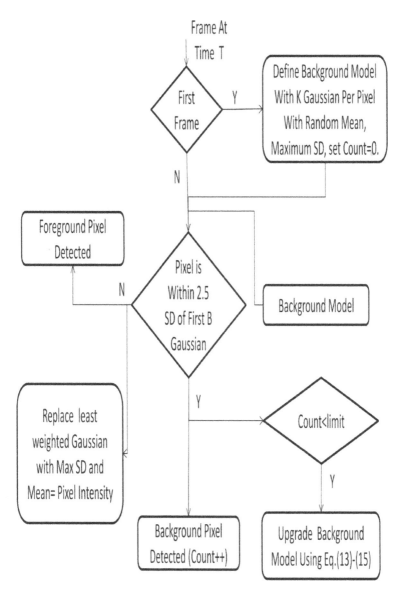

**Figure 3- 15 Basic Flow Chart Of GMM Algorithm**

In practice also mixture of Gaussian in used. The basic flow of object detection using GMM is shown in figure 3-14. From [8-12] we can write that the basic idea of this is to define k Gaussian distribution for a pixel to represent its state. The pixel is separated as foreground pixel if it does not match with background Gaussians and then they can be grouped using connected component analysis. Generally value of k is defined between 3-5. If the pixel value is represented as $X_t$, we can write the probability of pixel in terms of k Gaussian equation.

$$f(X_t = x) = \sum_{i=1}^{k} \omega_{i,t} \ \eta(x/\mu_{i,t}, \Sigma_{i,t}) \tag{10}$$

Where,

$$\eta(X_t/\mu_{i,t}, \Sigma_{i,t}) = \frac{1}{(2\pi)^{\frac{n}{2}} \ |\Sigma_{i,t}|^{\frac{1}{2}}} \ e^{-\frac{1}{2}(X_t - \mu_{i,t})^T \Sigma_{i,t}(X_t - \mu_{i,t})}$$

$\eta(X_t/\mu_{i,t}, \Sigma_{i,t})$ is the ith Gaussian distribution at t time, $\mu_{i,t}$ is a mean, $\Sigma_{i,t}$ is covariance matrix and $\omega_{i,t}$ is mean of weight of ith Gaussian distribution and it will also satisfy equation:

$$\sum_{i=1}^{k} \omega_{i,t} \ - 1 \tag{11}$$

For simplicity we can assume that each channel of color image is independent. So, we can simply write.

$$\Sigma_{i,t} = \delta_{i,t}^2 I \tag{12}$$

If a new pixel value $X_{t+1}$ can be matched with the exiting Gaussians using the equation (16) than weight of all Gaussians mean and variance can be updated using equations 13, 14 & 15.

$$\omega_{i,t} = (1 - \beta)\omega_{i,t-1} + \beta \tag{13}$$

$$\mu_{i,t} = (1 - \rho)\mu_{i,t-1} + \rho\mu_{i,t} \tag{14}$$

$$\delta_{i,t}^2 = (1-\rho)\delta_{i,t-1}^2 + \rho(I_t - \mu_{i,t})^2 \qquad (15)$$

Where,

$$\rho = \beta\eta\big(I_t/\mu_{i,t-1}, \delta_{i,t-1}\big)$$

If $X_{t+1}$ do not match with any of the existing k Gaussian than the probably distribution with lowest weight is replaced by new distribution with $\mu_{i,t} = X_{t+1}$, a high variance and low weight. Then the first B distributions are chosen as background model,

$$B = srg_b^{min}(\sum_{k=1}^b \omega_k > T) \qquad (16)$$

Where, T is predefined threshold which is a minimum weight for representing a background. If a current pixel background is matches with any one of this B distribution it consider as a background pixel.

For example if we consider gray image and set k=5, we will observe the history of a pixel something like as shown in figure 3-15. If we choose B is three than the distribution with largest three weights become background model which is shown as red color in figure-3-16.

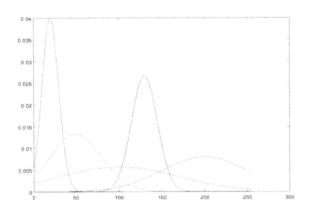

**Figure 3-16 Representation of history of a pixel in k=5 distributions [21]**

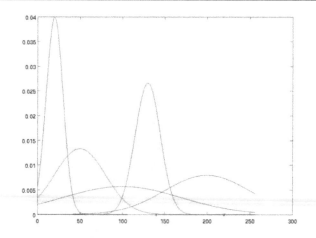

**Figure 3-17 B=3 distribution with largest weight [21]**

As shown in figure 3-17, we have calculated foreground mask for input frame i using mode k=3, SD = 9, Alpha = 0.05 and Threshold T = 0.3. As there are separate threshold for each pixel detected foreground mask is good compare to other methods explain earlier. As from figure 3-14, we have define count and limit variable to improve result of GMM. As now whenever pixel detected as a background pixel background model is updated as SD is reduced and position of mean updates. As if it continues for long time SD will become very small. And as we have observed that after some time it will detect pixel as a foreground even if it's intensity value is very near to mean value. So foreground is only detected true for some time and then output is ruined. To solve this problem we have introduce count and limit variable. If pixel will detect as background continuously count will increase and SD get updated until count reaches limit. After that no updating take place until count get reset and count only get reset when pixel found as a foreground.

The advantages of GMM is that we can decide threshold for every pixel and threshold is automatically updated. Secondly, this method allows object to become the part of background without destroying existing background model and GMM does a fast recovery compare to other methods explain above. The main disadvantage of GMM is that it is very sensitive to sudden light changes.

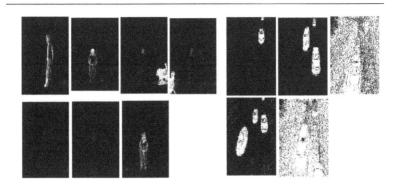

**Figure 3-18 Output Of GMM With Alpha 0.05, SD 9 and Threshold 0.3**

## 3.8 Eigenbackground

The next method is Eigen Background method. This approach is based on Eigen value decomposition. Principle component analysis (PCA) is the method which is commonly used to mold the background by significantly reduces the dimension of data.

Principle component [15-17] analysis is a statistical procedure which is useful in a dimensionality reduction by obtaining the principal components of the multi-dimensional data. The first principal component with the highest Eigen value is the linear combination of the original dimensions that has the highest variability.

For example, consider the figure 3-15, suppose that the triangles represent a two variable data set which we have measured in the X-Y coordinate system. U axis represents the direction in which data variation is maximum, so U is called first principal direction. Same way second most important direction is the V axis which is orthogonal to U axis. If we place the U-V axis system at the mean of the data it gives us a compact representation. If we plot each data point of (X,Y) coordinate into corresponding (U,V) coordinate system than the data is de-correlated that means the co-variance between the U and V variables is zero. For a given set of data, principal component analysis finds the axis system defined by the principal directions of variance (i.e. the U-V axis system in figure 3-10). The directions U and V are called the principal components.

3.8.1 Computing Principle Components

Principle component [17] founds by calculating the eigenvectors and eigenvalues of the data covariance matrix. This process is equivalent to finding the axis system in which the co-variance matrix is diagonal. The eigenvector with the largest eigenvalue is the direction of greatest variation, the one with the second largest eigenvalue is the (orthogonal) direction with the next highest variation and so on. To see how the computation is done we will give a brief review on eigenvectors / eigenvalues.

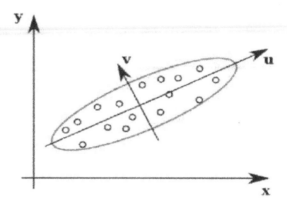

Figure 3-19  PCA for Data Representation [17]

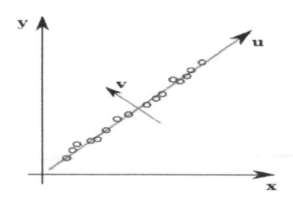

Figure 3-20  PCA for Dimension Reduction [17]

Let A is a nxn matrix. Then the eigenvalues of A are define as the roots of: Determinant(A-$\lambda$I) = |A-$\lambda$I | = 0; Where I is identity matrix of nxn. This equation is called the characteristic equation (or characteristic polynomial) and has n roots. Let $\lambda$ be an eigenvalue of A. Then there exists a vector X such that:

$AX = \lambda X$

The vector X is called an eigenvector of A associated with the eigenvalue $\lambda$. Notice that there is no unique solution for X in the above equation. It is a direction vector only and can be scaled to any magnitude. To find a numerical solution for X we need to set one of its elements to an arbitrary value, say 1, which gives us a set of simultaneous equations to solve for the other elements. If there is no solution repeat the process with another element. Ordinarily normalize the final values so that X has length one, that is $X * X^T = 1$.

Suppose a 3 x 3 matrix A with eigenvectors x1, x2, x3 and eigen values $\lambda$1, $\lambda$2, $\lambda$3 so:

Ax1=$\lambda$1x1

Ax2=$\lambda$2x2

Ax3=$\lambda$3x3

Putting the eigenvectors as the columns of a matrix gives:

$$A[x1\ x2\ x3] = [x1\ x2\ x3] \begin{bmatrix} \lambda1 & 0 & 0 \\ 0 & \lambda2 & 0 \\ 0 & 0 & \lambda3 \end{bmatrix}$$

Writing:

$\Phi= [x1\ x2\ x3]$

$$\Lambda = \begin{bmatrix} \lambda1 & 0 & 0 \\ 0 & \lambda2 & 0 \\ 0 & 0 & \lambda3 \end{bmatrix}$$

Writing:

Give matrix equation:

$$A\Phi = \Phi \, \Lambda$$

Normalized the eigenvectors to unit magnitude and they are orthogonal so:

$$\Phi\phi^T \;=\; \Phi\phi^T = I$$

Which means that:

$$\Phi\phi^T \, A \, \Phi = \Lambda \quad \text{and} \quad A = \Phi \, \Lambda \, \Phi^T$$

Now let consider how this applies to the covariance matrix in the PCA process. Let be $\Sigma$ an n x n covariance matrix. There is an orthogonal n x n matrix $\Phi$ whose columns are eigenvectors of $\Sigma$ and a diagonal matrix are $\Lambda$ whose diagonal elements are the eigen values of $\Sigma$ such that $\Phi^T \, \Sigma \, \Phi = \Lambda$.

The matrix of eigenvectors $\Phi$ as a linear transformation which, transforms data points in the [X,Y] axis system into the [U,V] axis system. In the general case the linear transformation given by $\Phi$ transforms the data points into a data set where the variables are uncorrelated. The correlation matrix of the data in the new coordinate system $\Lambda$ is which has zeros in all the off diagonal elements.

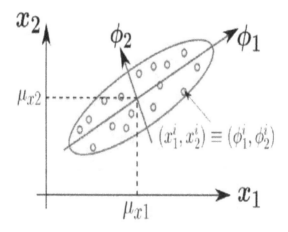

**Figure 3-21 The PCA Transformation [17]**

Figure 3-17 gives a geometric illustration of the process in two dimensions. Using all the data points we find the mean values of the variables ($\mu1,\mu2$) and the covariance matrix $\Sigma$ which is a 2x2 matrix in this case. If we calculate the eigenvectors of the co-variance matrix we get the direction vectors indicated by $\Phi1$ and $\Phi2$. Putting the two eigenvectors as columns in the matrix $\Phi=[\ \Phi1,\ \Phi2]$ , create a transformation matrix which takes our data points from the [x1,x2] axis system to the axis [$\Phi1,\ \Phi2$] system with the equation:

$$p\Phi = (px-\ \mu1).\ \Phi$$

Where px is any point in the [x1, x2] axis system $\mu x = (\mu x1, \mu x2)$ is the data mean, and $p\Phi$ is the coordinate of the point in the [$\Phi1,\ \Phi2$] axis system.

Thus, using PCA we can represent M dimensional data in to N dimension, where N<M. So, using these we can reduce computational complexity. PCA can be applied on M frames and it is much faster than Gaussian Mixture Model. The method can be summarized from [8] and [18-24] as follow.

- Training set of m images of size NxN are represented by vectors of size $N^2$. So, Now, this two dimensional vector is changed to one dimensional vector $\Gamma i$.

- Each image is represented by the vector $\Gamma i$.

- Average image is calculated by
$$\Psi = (\Gamma1 + \Gamma2 + \Gamma3 + \Gamma4+..... \Gamma M)/M \qquad (17)$$

- Each face differs from the average by $\Phi i= \Gamma i - \Psi$ ,which is called mean centered Image.

- A covariance matrix is constructed as: $C =AA^T$, where A = [$\Phi1, \Phi2, ...., \Phi M$]

- Eigen vectors corresponding to this covariance matrix is needed to be calculated. A*Xi is the Eigen vector and $\lambda i$ is the Eigen value.

- Only best N eigenvectors stored in an eigenvector matrix thus eigenvector matrix size will reduce and Eigen vectors of the covariance matrix $AA^T$ are AXi which is denoted by Ui.

- For every new image I can be projected on   Eigen space $I' = U^T(I - \Psi)$; where $(I-\Psi)$ is the mean centered image.
- $I'$ is converted back to the image space as $I'' = U\ I' + \Psi$. Because Eigen space is suited for   static part of seen. So, $I''$ will not contain any moving object.
- So, we can found foreground object using equation

$$|I - I''| > T \tag{18}$$

Where, T is user define threshold.

By, using this step we can able to obtain foreground pixels and by connecting them we can locate foreground object.

Output of Eigen background method is shown in figure 3-18 with no adaption. Though, it is not much affected by lighting changes but it is only useful for small & medium object. Also it uses Principle Component Analysis, so method is faster than GMM.

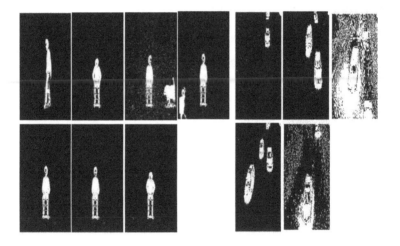

**Figure 3-18 Output Of Eigenbackground**

# CHAPTER 4

## COMPARISION OF BACKGROUND SUBTRACTION ALGORITHMS

In chapter 3 we have studied different kinds of Background Subtraction Algorithms and their experimental results. We have comment on their performance to obtain foreground and their advantages - disadvantages. In this section we have done comparative analysis[13],[25] of these algorithms by their speed to obtain foreground pixels and memory.

By using this output we can compare them as per memory requirement and speed of algorithm which is shown in table 1. Here, values of speed are the observation that we have experience during our output evaluation for each frame. It may not be same for different conditions. Memory requirement specify here is for calculation of foreground for one pixel.

TABLE 4-1 Memory Requirement Per Pixel And Execution Speed Observed For Particular Video Series Per Frame

| Method | Memory | Speed |
|---|---|---|
| Simple BSS | 1 | .05T |
| Mean Filtering | N | 1.5T (5 Training Signal) |
| | | 2.5T (15 Training Signal) |
| Median Filtering | N | 2.3T (5 Training Signal) |
| | | 3.18T (15 Training Signal) |
| W4 Sysytem | N+3 | 0.1T |
| Frame differencing | 1 | .05T |
| SGM | 1 | 2.5T |
| GMM | K | 8T |
| Eigenbackground | N | .15T |

From the table 4-1, Simple Background Subtraction require to store only one frame, which is reference frame only. So per pixel memory requirement to find foreground is 1 and observed speed in our experiment is 0.05T, where T is one time unit. For Mean Filtering we have to calculate mean of last N frames. So, per pixel memory requirement to find foreground is N, where N is no of training signal required to build background model. Also we require N frames in Median filtering as well. We have done experiments for N=5 & N=15, for that the speed of operation for Mean Filtering is 1.5T & 2.5T and for Median Filtering speed is 2.3T & 3.18T. In W4 System we require training sequence of N frames from which we calculate maximum intensity matrix and minimum intensity matrix. So we require to store N frames, minimum intensity matrix , maximum intensity matrix and frame at time t-1. So, total storage pixel required for one pixel analysis is N+3. The speed observed is 0.1T. Next method is Frame Differencing, in which frame at t-1 must be stored. So memory requirement is 1 & speed observed is 0.05T. In Single Gaussian Model, we maintain 1gaussian per pixel to detect the current pixel is foreground or background pixel, so memory requirement is 1 and speed is approximate 2.5T. In GMM we maintain K no of Gaussians per pixel to find background mode, so memory consumption increases to K, where K is number of Gaussians in GMM. To maintain and update whole bunch of parameters it consumes more time near 8T. The last method is Eigenbackground, in this method we have to create eigen space using N number of frames only once, but still it requires storage is N. Though it deals with frame which is reduced from its original size, it consumes less processing time like 0.15T.

# CHAPTER 5

## OPTICAL FLOW

The optical flow methods [26-29] try to calculate the motion between two image frames which are taken at times t and $t + \Delta t$ at every pixel position. These methods are called differential since they are based on local Taylor series approximations of the image signal; that is, they use partial derivatives with respect to the spatial and temporal coordinates.

For a 2 dimensional case at pixel location (x,y,t) with intensity I(x,y,t) will have moved by $\Delta x$, $\Delta y$ and $\Delta t$ between the two image frames, and the following brightness constancy constraint can be given:

$$I(x, y, t) = I(x + \Delta x, y + \Delta y, t + \Delta t)$$

Assuming the movement to be small, the image constraint at I(x,y,t) with Taylor series can be apply as follow.

$$I(x + \Delta x, y + \Delta y, t + \Delta t) = I(x, y, t) + \frac{\partial I}{\partial x} \Delta x + \frac{\partial I}{\partial y} \Delta y + \frac{\partial I}{\partial t} \Delta t$$

From these equations we can write,

$$\frac{\partial I}{\partial x} \Delta x + \frac{\partial I}{\partial y} \Delta y + \frac{\partial I}{\partial t} \Delta t = 0$$

$$\frac{\partial I}{\partial x} \frac{\Delta x}{\Delta t} + \frac{\partial I}{\partial y} \frac{\Delta y}{\Delta t} + \frac{\partial I}{\partial t} \frac{\Delta t}{\Delta t} = 0$$

which results in

$$\frac{\partial I}{\partial x} V_x + \frac{\partial I}{\partial y} V_y + \frac{\partial I}{\partial t} = 0$$

where $V_x$ and $V_y$ are the x and y components of the velocity or optical flow of I(x,y,t) and $\frac{\partial I}{\partial x}$, $\frac{\partial I}{\partial y}$ and $\frac{\partial I}{\partial t}$ are the derivatives of the image at (x,y,t) in the corresponding directions. Thus,

$$I_x V_x + I_y V_y = -I_t \tag{5.1}$$

This is an equation in two unknowns and cannot be solved as such. This is known as the aperture problem of the optical flow algorithms. To find the optical flow another set of equations is needed, given by some additional constraint. All optical flow methods introduce additional conditions for estimating the actual flow.

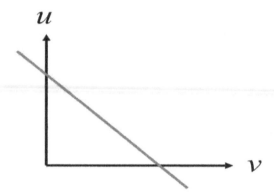

**Figure 5 - 1 Optical Flow Constrain**

If we plot equation 5.1, we found the constrain diagram in figure 5-1 ,if we put u = 0 and v=0, we got strait line as mentioned in figure. So, optical flow (u,v) is lies on this strait line but where we cannot say. So we require some other additional equation to solve this aperture problem.

## 5.1 The Smoothness Constraint [30]

If every point of the brightness pattern can move independently, there is little hope of recovering the velocities. More commonly we view opaque objects of finite size undergoing rigid motion or deformation. In this case neighbouring points on the objects have similar velocities and the velocity field of the brightness patterns in the image varies smoothly almost everywhere. Discontinuities in flow can be expected where one object occludes another. An algorithm based on a smoothness constraint is likely to have difficulties with occluding edges as a result. One way to express the additional constraint is to minimize the square of the magnitude of the gradient of the optical flow velocity:

$$(\frac{\partial u}{\partial x})^2 + (\frac{\partial u}{\partial y})^2 \ \ and \ \ (\frac{\partial v}{\partial x})^2 + (\frac{\partial v}{\partial y})^2$$

Another measure of the smoothness of the optical flow field is the sum of the squares of the Laplacians of the x- and y-components of the flow.

Laplacian of u and v define as

$$\Delta^2 u = \frac{\partial^2 u}{\partial x^2} + \frac{\partial^2 u}{\partial y^2} \ \ and \ \ \Delta^2 v = \frac{\partial^2 v}{\partial x^2} + \frac{\partial^2 v}{\partial y^2}$$

In simple situations, both Laplacians are zero.

## 5.2 Determining Optical Flow Using Horn - Schunck Algorithm[30]

Horn - Schunck algorithm follows two criterion. First, optical flow is smooth given by

$$F_s(u,v) = \iint \left(u_x^2 + u_y^2\right) + \left(v_x^2 + v_y^2\right) dx \, dy \qquad (5.2)$$

and the second criterion is Optical flow constraint equation given by

$$F_h(u,v) = \iint (I_x V_x + I_y V_y + I_t)^2 dx \, dy \qquad (5.3)$$

So, we combine this error function and try to minimize it. Here, double integration means this operation follows for all pixels in whole frame. So, our equation is given as:

$$F(u,v) = \iint \left(I_x V_x + I_y V_y + I_t\right)^2 + \alpha^2 (\left|\left|\nabla u\right|\right|^2 + \left|\left|\nabla v\right|\right|^2) dx \, dy \qquad (5.4)$$

By minimising this equation and after apply Variation calculus we get a pair of second order differential equations that can be solved iteratively.

$$u^{k+1} = \bar{u}^k - \frac{I_x \left[ I_x \bar{u}^k + I_y \bar{v}^k + I_t \right]}{\alpha^2 + I_x^2 + I_y^2}$$

$$\qquad (5.5)$$

$$v^{k+1} = \bar{v}^k - \frac{I_y \left[ I_x \bar{u}^k + I_y \bar{v}^k + I_t \right]}{\alpha^2 + I_x^2 + I_y^2}$$

## 5.3 Estimation Of Classical Partial Derivatives

This section presents the estimation process of the classical derivatives of image intensity or brightness from the image sequence. The brightness of each pixel is constant along its motion trajectory in the image sequence. The relationship in continuous images sequence will be taken into account to estimate the original intensity for a gradient constraint. Let I(x,y,t) denote the gradient intensity (brightness) of point (x,y) in the images at time t. In each image sequence, Ix, Iy, and It are computed for each pixel:

$$I_x = \tfrac{1}{4} \{ I_{x,y+1,t} - I_{x,y,t} + I_{x+1,y+1,t} - I_{x+1,y,t} + I_{x,y+1,t+1} - I_{x,y,t+1} + I_{x+1,y+1,t+1} - I_{x+1,y,t+1} \},$$

$$I_y = \tfrac{1}{4} \{ I_{x+1,y,t} - I_{x,y,t} + I_{x+1,y+1,t} - I_{x,y+1,t} + I_{x+1,y,t+1} - I_{x,y,t+1} + I_{x+1,y+1,t+1} - I_{x,y+1,t+1} \},$$

$$I_t = \tfrac{1}{4} \{ I_{x,y,t+1} - I_{x,y,t} + I_{x+1,y,t+1} - I_{x+1,y,t} + I_{x,y+1,t+1} - I_{x,y+1,t} + I_{x+1,y+1,t+1} - I_{x+1,y+1,t} \}.$$

For example we can consider following case:

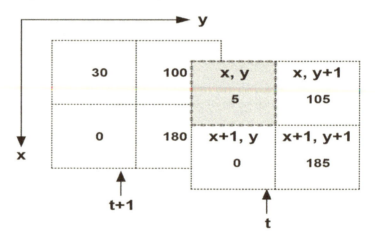

**Figure 5 - 2 Partial Derivatives Of Image Brightness At Point (X, Y)[30]**

$$I_x = ((105 - 5) + (185 - 0) + (100 - 3\ 0) + (180 - 0)) / 4 = 133.75$$

$$I_y = ((0 - 5) + (185 - 105) + (0 - 30) + (180 - 100)) / 4 = 31.25$$

$$I_t = ((30 - 5) + (0 - 0) + (100 - 105) + (180 - 185)) / 4 = 3.75$$

Estimation of partial derivatives on BFB kernel    Barron et al. (1994) proposed performance evaluation over many algorithms of optical flow and modification of some of the variant variables. We focus on the kernel of mask coefficient for gradient estimation which is the core functional of the HS algorithms. The gradient estimation kernel of the BFB model uses 4-point central differences for differentiation defined as

$$I_x = 1/12 \{-1 * I_{x,y-2} + 8 * I_{x,y-1} + 0 * I_{x,y} - 8 * I_{x,y+1} + 1 * I_{x,y+2}\},$$

$$I_y = 1/12 \{-1 * I_{x-2,y} + 8 * I_{x-1,y} + 0 * I_{x,y} - 8 * I_{x+1,y} + 1 * I_{x+2,y}\},$$

$$I_t = 1/12 \{-1 * I_{x,y,t-2} + 8 * I_{x,y,t-1} + 0 * I_{x,y,t} - 8 * I_{x,y,t+1} + 1 * I_{x,y,t+2}\}$$

| 1/12 | -1 | 8 | 0 | -8 | 1 |
|------|----|---|---|----|----|

**Figure 5 - 3 BFB Kernel**

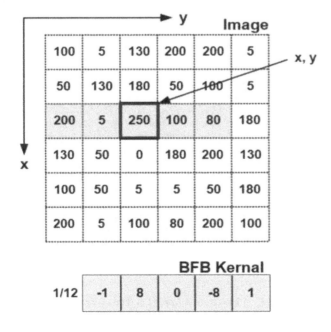

**Figure 5 - 4 BFB Kernel Apply For X Direction Displacement [30]**

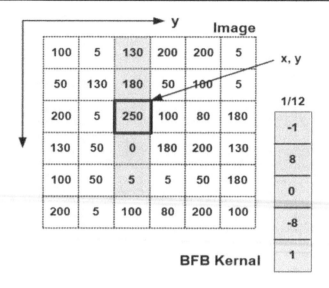

Figure 5 - 5 BFB Kernel Apply For Y Direction Displacement[30]

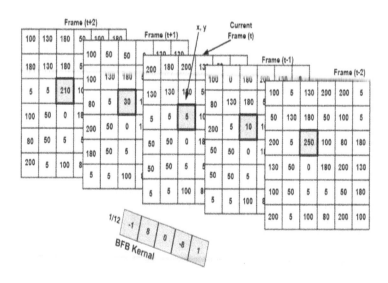

Figure 5 - 6 BFB Kernel Apply For Time Displacement[30]

It is known that in most situations of motion estimation one may use only two frames to calculate It as shown in Fig. 5-4 to 5-6. As a result of using the BFB kernel, it presents more stability of original gradient estimation than the result of performance evaluation in Barron. From above figures we can solve for one pixel as:

Ix(2,2) = (-1 x 200 + 8 x 5 + 0 x 250 – 8 x 100 + 1 x 80) / 12 = -73.33

Iy(2,2) = (-1 x 130 + 8 x 180 + 0 x 250 – 8 x 0 + 1 x 5) / 12 = 109.58

It(2,2) = (-1 x 210 + 8 x 30 + 0 x 5 – 8 x 10 + 1 x 250) / 12 = 16.66

An illustration of gradient the smoothness weight (α) is iteratively presented :

$$u^{k+1} = \bar{u}^k - \frac{I_x \left[ I_x \bar{u}^k + I_y \bar{v}^k + I_t \right]}{\alpha^2 + I_x^2 + I_y^2}$$

$$v^{k+1} = \bar{v}^k - \frac{I_y \left[ I_x \bar{u}^k + I_y \bar{v}^k + I_t \right]}{\alpha^2 + I_x^2 + I_y^2}$$

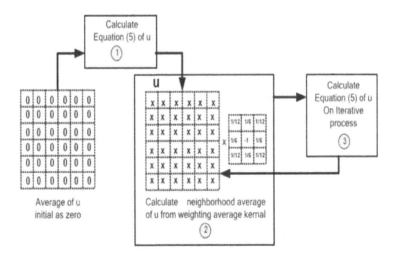

**Figure 5 - 7 An Illustration Of The Iterative Minimization Process For U Where Steps 2 And 3 Are Iterative [30]**

where $\bar{u}^k$ and $\bar{v}^k$ denote horizontal and vertical neighbourhood, which initially are set to zero and then the weighted average of the value at neighboring points based on the kernel in Fig. 5-7 is applied for further iterations using Eq. 5.5. The smoothness weight (α) plays an important role where the brightness gradient is small, for which the suitable value should be determined.

## 5-4 Experiment Results

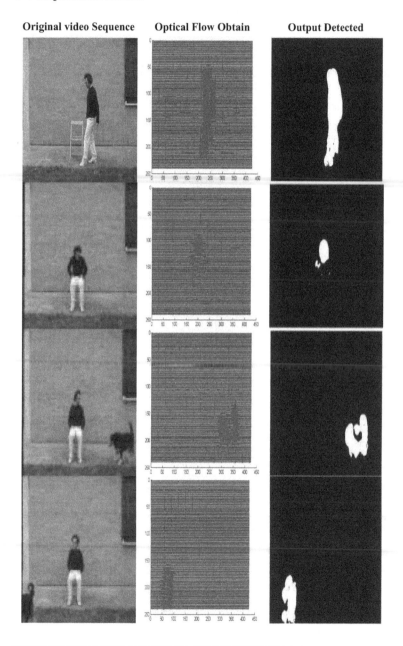

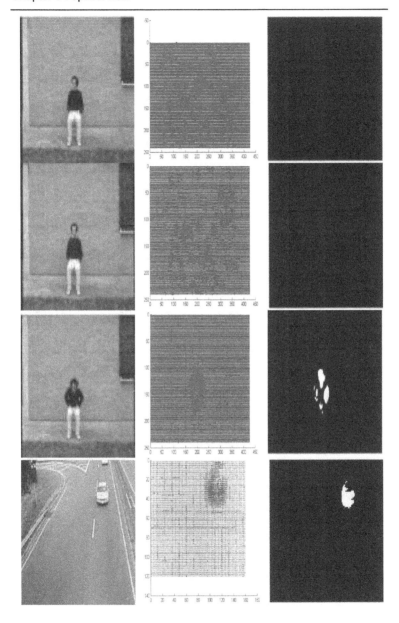

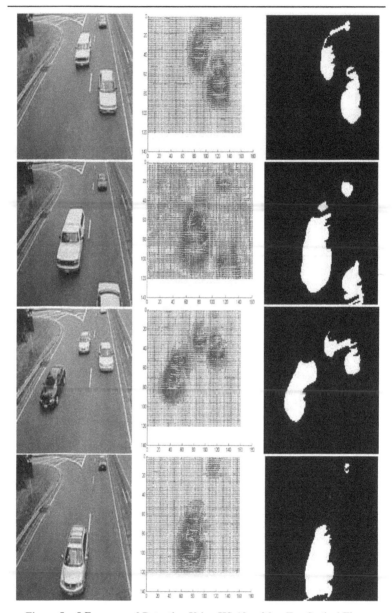

Figure 5 - 8 Foreground Detection Using HS Algorithm For Optical Flow

Figure 5-8 shows the optical flow vectors obtain using Horn - Schunck Algorithm. After applying threshold we can obtain fore ground. Here for these experiments we have used alpha = 50. As we can see that optical vectors are very less affected by the sudden lightening changes. So, we can use this results to improve our Background Subtraction Algorithms, which are very much sensitive to this effect. In the next chapter we have combine this techniques with our Background Subtraction technique.

# CHAPTER 6

## COMBINE GMM & OPTICAL FLOW

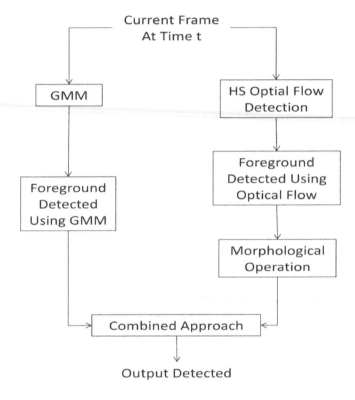

**Figure 6- 1 Block Diagram Of Combined Approach**

In the above chapters, we have studied different kinds of background subtraction techniques. We have observed that among all those methods GMM have good performance in foreground detection, but it is very sensitive with illumination changes. So when ever lightening changes occur we lost our object. We also studied Optical Flow method for moving segmentation. Though it is not good at boundary detection but it will perform comparatively good to detect movement in illumination changes. As from [31-35] we can improve GMM with many ways. In this project we have tried to improve GMM algorithms by combining GMM with Optical Flow. So,

**Original video Sequence**     **Output Of GMM**     **Final Output Detected**

Figure 6- 2 Output Of Combined Method Compare With GMM Method

we can remove each other's negative points. As shown in figure 6-1, we can combine these two algorithms and obtain accurate output.

In the figure 6-2, we have represent detected output for combined approach. Here, we have compared it's output to GMM method. One can see that moving object are clearly detected in combine approach while it is not detected in GMM when sudden lightening changes. Here, we have used alpha = 50 in optical flow and k=3, Threshold = .3, SD = 9 and alpha = .05 for GMM and execution time observed during experiments are around 8T.

# CHAPTER 7

## SHADOW DETECTION

In the field of moving object detection using background subtraction, there are many challenges which is explain in chapter 2. For foreground detection most of the time shadow of moving and static object is also detected as a foreground, which is cause of false detection of object. In this project we have used simple method based on HSV mode. HSV mode [36-38]is explain below.

### 7.1 HSV/HSI Mode (Hue Saturation Value/Intensity)

HSV stands for hue, saturation and value. Hue is one of the main properties of a color. It represents a pure color (without any tint or shade). A hue is an element of the color wheel.

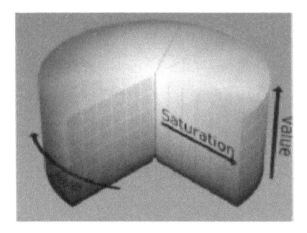

**Figure 7- 1 HSV Mode [39]**

Saturation is the difference of a color against its own brightness. The saturation of a color is determined by a combination of light intensity and how much it is distributed across the spectrum of different wavelengths. The purest color is achieved by using just one wavelength at a high intensity, such as in laser light. If the intensity drops, so does the saturation. Intensity is the brightness or dullness of a hue. One may lower the intensity by adding white or black. Many applications use the HSI color model. Machine vision uses HSI color space in identifying the color of different objects. Image processing applications such as histogram operations, intensity transformations and convolutions operate only on an intensity image. These operations are performed with much ease on an image in the HSI color space.

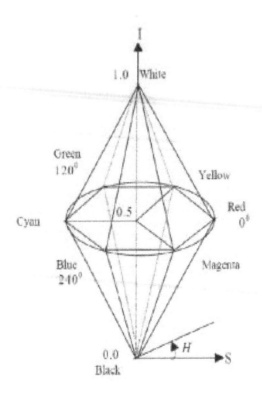

**Figure 7- 2 Double cone model of HSV mode [39]**

The hue (H) is represented as the angle, varying from 0 to 360. Saturation (S) corresponds to the radius, varying from 0 to 1. Intensity (I) varies along the z axis with 0 being black and 1 being white. When S = 0, color is a gray value of intensity 1. When S = 1, color is on the boundary of top cone base. The greater the saturation, the farther the color is from white/gray/black (depending on the intensity). Adjusting the hue will vary the color from red at 0o, through green at120o, blue at 240o, and back to red at 360o. When I = 0, the color is black and therefore H is undefined. When S= 0, the color is gray scale. H is also undefined in this case. By adjusting I, a color can be made darker or lighter. By maintaining S= 1 and adjusting I, shades of that color are created.

## 7.2 Shadow Detection

As we explain in [36-38] that shadow is created by the light cause false detection. To detect shadow we convert our image in HSV space because it is very sensitive to brightness levels of image. The shadow detection can be carried out using following equation.

$$S(x,y) = \begin{cases} 1 \ , \alpha_s \leq \dfrac{I_v(x,y)}{B_v(x,y)} \leq \beta_s \\ I_s(x,y) - B_s(x,y) \leq T_s \\ |I_H(x,y) - B_H(x,y)| \leq T_R \\ 0, else \end{cases} \qquad (18)$$

Where I(x,y) represents the current image, B(x,y) means background image. $T_s$ and $T_R$ represents threshold values for color and chrome. The value of $\beta_s$ is less than 1, because intensity of shadow region is lower than non-shadow image. Also, the saturation of shadow part is lower than non-shadow one. This HSV space can be carried out through GMM algorithm to remove shadows.

As shown in figure the detected shadow of given input image is shown in figure 4-3.

input frame

detected shadow

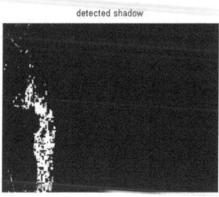

**Figure 7- 3 Output Of Shadow Detection**

(a) input image (b) detected shadow using HSV mode threshold

# CHAPTER 8

## CONCLUSION AND FUTURE WORK

In this thesis, we have studied different types of background subtractions algorithms. I have also done comparative analysis of all the algorithms. This paper gives very good idea about the techniques used for moving object detection using Background Subtraction method. I have experience that Simple method is the fastest among others but it is very sensitive to noise. From all the methods, W4 method is only useful for gray images. Accuracy of Frame differencing to detect object is totally depends on the speed of the moving object, so we cannot use it if speed of the object is less. Furthermore Running Gaussian average method performs faster than GMM and Eigen background. Also, running Gaussian average requires less memory than GMM and Eigen backgrounds because it uses single threshold for a pixel to decide whether it is foreground or background, also it is adaptive and fast because it have to update only two-three parameters to update background. If we compare the accuracy, GMM and Eigen backgrounds have good accuracy compare to other methods. But the GMM is more complex because it uses different threshold for each pixel and have many parameters to update, which reduces its speed and increases memory consumption. On the other hand, Eigen background which uses PCA so it will convert n dimension to m dimension (m<n), thus the complexity is reduce by (n - m). So, Eigen background is faster than GMM. so, we can select any method from above based on the environment, speed, memory requirement and accuracy of our system.

I have also performed combination of GMM and Optical Flow, from which we are able to improve object detection during illumination changes. This method is not improve performance in terms of speed and it also consumes slightly more memory. But it is good in terms of detection of moving object compare to other methods.

Thus, we can select any method from above based on the speed, memory requirement and accuracy of system. In future, we can improve performance of optical methods using pyramid approach and ultimately improve background subtraction methods. Also we can find moving objects with vibrating and moving camera.

# REFERENCES

[1]A. M. McIvor," Background Subtraction Techniques", Proc. of Image and Vision Computing,pp.155-163",2000.

[2]J Nascimento and J Marques, "Performance Evaluation Of Object Detection Algorithms For Video Surveillance", IEEE Transactions on Multimedia, Vol- 8 , Issue-4,pp-761-774,Aug 2006.

[3]K Gupta1, A Kulkarni,"Implementation of an Automated Single Camera Object Tracking System Using Frame Differencing, and Dynamic Template Matching", CISSE 07 Co-Sponsored by IEEE,pp 245-250, Dec 2007.

[4]K Jadav, M .Lokhandwala, A Gharge," Vision Based Moving Object Detection And Tracking",National Conference on Recent Trends in Engineering & Technology,pp.13-14, May 2011

[5]K Joshi, D Thakore ,"A Survey on Moving Object Detection and Tracking in Video Surveillance System", , International Journal of Soft Computing and Engineering, Vol-2, Issue-3, pp 44-48, July 2012.

[6]"Experiment Video Sequence"
Available : http://imagelab.ing.unimore.it/visor/video_details.asp?idvideo=45

[7]I Haritaoglu, D Harwood, and L Davis, "W4: Real-Time Surveillance Of People And Their Activities", IEEE Trans. on Pattern Analysis and Machine Intelligence, vol. 22, no. 8, pp. 809-830, August 2000.

[8]M Piccardi,"Background Subtraction Techniques: A Review", IEEE International Conference on Systems, Man and Cybernetics, Vol-4, pp 3099-3104, 2004.

[9]X Song, J Chen, X Zhou,"A Robust Moving Objects Detection Based on Improved Gaussian Mixture Model", IEEE International Conference on Artificial Intelligence and Computational Intelligence, Vol.2, pp 54-58, 2010.

[10]Z Bian and X Dong,"Moving Object Detection Based on Improved Gaussian Mixture Model", 5th International Congress on Image and Signal Processing, pp 109-112,2012.

[11]H Fu, H Ma and A Ming"EGMM: An Enhanced Gaussian Mixture Model For Detecting Moving Objects With Intermittent Stop", IEEE International Conference on Multimedia and Expo (ICME), pp 1-6, 2011

[12]C Stauffer and W Grimson, "Adaptive Background Mixture Models For Real-Time Tracking,", IEEE CVPR, Vol.2, June 1999.

[13]"Background Subtraction Algorithms"
Available:http://www.cs.utexas.edu/~grauman/courses/fall2009/slides /lecture9_background.pdf

[14]C Wren, A Azarhayejani, T. Darrell, and A.P. Pentland, "Pfinder: real-time tracking of the human body", IEEE Trans. on Patfern Anal. and Machine Infell., vol. 19, Issue. 7, pp. 780-785, 1997.

[15]N Oliver, B Rosario, and A Pentland, "A Bayesian Computer Vision System For Modeling Human Interactions", IEEE Trans. on Patfern Anal. and Machine Zntell., vol. 22, Issue. 8, pp. 831-843, 2000.

[16]C Zhang ,A Pan, S Zheng, X Cao,"Motion Object Detection Of Video Based On Principal Component Analysis", IEEE International Conference on Machine Learning and Cybernetics, Vol-5,pp 3938-3943, 2008.

[17]Jon Shlens,"A Tutorial On Principal Component Analysis"
Available: www.cs.princeton.edu/picasso/mats/PCA-Tutorial-Intuition_jp.pdf

[18]D Maniciu, P Meer "Mean shift: A Robust Approach Toward Feature Space Analysis", IEEE Trans. Patt. Analy. Mach. Intell. Vol-24, Issue- 5, pp 603–619, August 2002.

[19]B Moore," Principal Component Analysis In Linear Systems: Controllability, Observability, And Model Reduction",IEEE Transactions on Automatic Control, Volume:26 , Issue: 1, PP-17-32, 06 January 2003.

[20]H Hotelling , "Simplified Calculation Of Principal Components", Psychometrica, vol. 1, pp.27 -35,1936.

[21]A. Elgammal, D Hanvood, L Davis, "Non- Parametric Model For Background Subtraction", Proc. ECCV 2000, pp. 751-767, June 2000

[22]C Wang, L Lan, Y Zhang, M Gu, "Face Recognition Based on Principle ComponentAnalysis and Support Vector Machine", 3rd IEEE International workshop on Intel. System and Application, pp 1-4,2011.

[23]H Zhipeng, Y Wang, Y Tian, T Huang"Selective Eigenbackgrounds Method For Background Subtraction In Crowed Scenes",18th IEEE International Conference on Image Processing,Issue-1522-4880,pp3277-3280,2011.

[24]M. Seki, T Wada, H Fujiwara, K Sumi, "Background Subtraction Based On Cooccurrence Of Image Variations", Proc. CVPR 2003, Vol. 2, pp. 65-72, 2003.

[25]Y. Benezeth, P Jodoin "Comparative Study of Background Subtraction Algorithms", Journal of Electronic Imaging, vol-9, pp 033003-033003-12, July 2010.

[26]M Enric, J S´anchez, D Kondermann,"Horn–Schunck Optical Flow with a Multi-Scale Strategy", Image Processing On Line, 3, pp. 151–172, 2013.

[27]B Horn and B.G Schunck, "Determining Optical Flow", in Artificial Intelligence Vol: 17, pp. 185-204,1981.

[28]"Optical - Flow"
Available : www.people.csail.mit.edu/bkph/articles/Fixed_Flow.pdf

[29]"Optical - Flow"
Available:www.inf.u-szeged.hu/~kato/teaching/computervision/08-OpticalFlow.pdf

[30]D Kesrarat and V Patanavijit,"Tutorial of Motion Estimation Based on Horn-Schunk Optical Flow Algorithm in MATLAB", AU J.T. 15(1), pp8-16, Jul. 2011

[31]K.Hawari, W.Samsudin, M.Hamid, "Motion Detection for PC based on Security System by using Optical Flow", International General On Advance Science Engineering Information Technology, Vol.2 , pp 101-104, 2012

[32]H Fradi, J Dugelay,"Robust Foreground Segmentation Using Improved Gaussian Mixture Model and Optical Flow", International Conference on Informatics, Electronics & Vision (ICIEV),pp- 248 - 253, May 2012.

[33]Y Li, X Chang-zhen "Moving Object Detection Based on Edged Mixture Gaussian Models", IEEE International Workshop on Intelligent Systems and Applications, pp 1-5, May 2009.

[34]H Zeng and S Lai, "Adaptive foreground object extraction for real-time video surveillance with lighting variations," IEEE International Conference on Acoustics, Speech, and Signal Processing, vol. 1, pp. 1201– 1204, 2007.

[35]D Lee, "Effective gaussian mixture learning for video background subtraction," IEEE Transactions on Pattern Recognition and Machine Intelligence, vol. 27, pp. 827–832, 2005

[36]S Zhu, Z Guo ,L Ma," Shadow removal with background difference method based on shadow posotion and edge attributes", Journal on Image and Video Processing, December ,2012

[37] Y Liu , W Zhao, "Shadow Suppression Based on Adaptive Gaussian Mixture Model",National Conference on Information Technology and Computer Science , 2012

[38]S Surkutlawar, R Kulkarni"Shadow Suppression using RGB and HSV Color Space in Moving Object Detection", International Journal of Advanced Computer Science and Applications, Vol. 4, pp 164-169, 2013

[39]"HSV Mode Image" Available: http://www.google.co.in/imgres

www.ingramcontent.com/pod-product-compliance
Lightning Source LLC
La Vergne TN
LVHW092353060326
832902LV00008B/1003